THE LITTLE BOOK OF HAPPINESS

AVA CADWELL

THE LITTLE BOOK OF HAPPINESS

AVA CADWELL

I hope this book
inspires you
to follow your dreams,
reach your goals,
and find happiness.

Keep this book handy
for inspiration.
May it help you
inspire others, too.

Ava

BREAK
THE RULES

LOVE

more

WORRY

less

IT'S INSPIRING TO BE DIFFERENT. IT'S BORING TO BE THE SAME.

SMILES AND KINDNESS OPEN ALL DOORS.

AND IF YOU
FALL?

JUST STAND UP AND WALK AGAIN

KEEP

trying

life's
obstacles

= THEY TEACH US SOME
IMPORTANT LIFE LESSONS

STAY FOCUSED ON YOUR GOAL.

BELIEVE
IN A
BETTER
FUTURE.
BELIEVE
IN A
BETTER
WORLD.

Believe

JUST DO WHAT
YOU ENJOY
DOING

the most
important
things in
life are not
material

BE
THANKFUL.

THINGS COULD BE WORSE.

*THE FUTURE
LOOKS
PROMISING.*

MEDI
TATE

LO
VE

YOURSELF

SEIZE THE DAY
EVERY DAY.

Believe it.
Dream
about it.
Feel it.
It will
happen.

BE PATIENT

Keep on thinking

POSITIVE

If you
can't
change it,
accept it.

You are
wonderful!

SPEAK OUT.
STAND UP FOR
YOUR BELIEFS.
BATTLE AGAINST
THE ODDS.
DISCOVER YOUR
INNER REBEL.
SHAKE UP
THE WORLD.

persevere

A GREAT ATTITUDE LEADS TO A GREAT DAY. A BAD ATTITUDE LEADS TO A BAD DAY.

treat everyone

ALIKE

mistakes
might
lead you
to the
right path

Give love,
lots of
love!

Sometimes
things don't go
according
to plan.

AND THAT'S OKAY.

EVERYTHING
WILL CLEAR UP
SOON.

RELAX.

THE POWER IS
WITHIN YOU

**IT TAKES TIME FOR
GOOD THINGS
TO HAPPEN**

Smile!

NO MATTER WHAT HAPPENS IN LIFE, JUST KEEP WALKING.

SPEND MORE TIME IN

NATURE

LAUGH.

LOVE YOUR
life.

LIVE WITH
love.

BE
CREATIVE.

play.

No one is perfect.

THERE'S
ALWAYS PLAN
B, C, D, E, F, G,
H, I, J, K, L, M,
N, O, P, Q, R,
S, T, U, V, W,
X, Y AND Z.

take a break

JUST BE YOU.

STAY POSITIVE.

be kind.

miracles
do happen

TOMORROW
WILL BE A
BETTER DAY.

In the end,
everything
will be
okay.

LISTEN
MORE.
SPEAK
LESS.

Put a smile on
your face and the
whole world will
smile at you!

**BE BOLD.
BE BRAVE.
BE CONFIDENT.**

DON'T LIVE
THEIR LIFE.
LIVE YOUR LIFE.

SOMETHING WONDERFUL MIGHT HAPPEN TODAY.

Keep your eyes open!

Have faith things will be better.

Love
Eat
Dream

HAVE FUN

Bring
change
into your
life.

LIFE IS
WONDERFUL.
YOU ARE
WONDERFUL.
AND YOU CAN
DO WONDERFUL
THINGS IN LIFE.

NEVER CHANGE YOURSELF FOR ANYONE.

Be kind to
everyone,
and everyone
will be kind
to you.

STEP OUT
OF YOUR
COMFORT
ZONE

positive

vibes,

please!

There's no better time than the present time to love, work, exercise, laugh, hug, study, cook, watch a movie, do the laundry, walk the dog, read a book, knit, go shopping, and make dreams come true.

Intuition.
Trust it.

YOU
FAILED?
SO
WHAT?

Live in the
present
moment!

BE THIRSTY
FOR
KNOWLEDGE

challenge
yourself
to try
something
new today

eat, sleep and
read

BE NICE.

Forgive and
forget.

Keep
LEARNING

SING.

make it
happen

it's never
too late
to learn
a new skill

GIVE AND RECEIVE.

Every morning a
new opportunity
arises.
And with every
new opportunity
a new life
begins!

ONE STEP
AT A TIME

TRUST THE
PROCESS.

You just had
a bad day?
Forget it.
Tomorrow
is a new day.

WISDOM AND
KNOWLEDGE
COME WITH
DIFFICULTIES,
NOT AN EASY
LIFE.

IF YOU WANT TO DO
SOMETHING DO IT

NOW

IT'S OKAY
TO CRY

FACE
YOUR FEARS.

You think
you're too
old to learn
salsa?

DO SOMETHING
TO GET CLOSER
TO YOUR DREAMS.

it's okay
to get lost

**AT LEAST
GIVE IT A TRY.**

Positivity leads to
happiness and joy.
Negativity
leads to worries.
Choose wisely
how you train
your brain to think.

Respect people.
Respect animals.
Respect
our home.

SLEEP.
NO BETTER
MEDICINE.

Spread love.
Spread smiles.

EMBRACE
LIFE'S
CHALLENGES

Every day is a new day
full of opportunities,
challenges, happy
moments, and bad
experiences.

Try to make each day
special and focus on the
positive things that can
bring joy and fulfillment
to your life.

Change

CHALLENGE
YOURSELF.
TAKE RISKS.
THAT'S HOW
YOU GROW.

you are where
you should be
right now...

enjoy the
journey!

DO.
FAIL.
TRY AGAIN.

Share your
happiness!

TAKE THE FIRST STEP. EVERYTHING ELSE WILL FOLLOW.

Believe in yourself.

Everything happens
when the time is right.

not happy with
life?
change it

Count your
blessings!

Never give up
on your
goals.

Never give up
on your
dreams.

DON'T JUST IMAGINE
A BETTER WORLD.

YOU HAVE
THE POWER
TO CREATE ONE.

TRAVEL

STAY POSITIVE.
BETTER DAYS
ARE COMING.

Peaceful mind.
Peaceful person.

Worried mind.
Worried person.

a new
life
begins
today